MW01174517

How to Rewrite Fables in a TUM Way

w w w . t - u - m . n e t

Methodology by Peter Feng, assisted by Andrew Feng

Comic Dialogues by Andrew Feng, assisted by Peter Feng

Comic Sketches by Andrew Feng

Comic Digital Ink by Peter Feng

6 New Stories by Andrew Feng, assisted by Peter Feng

Citation by Peter Feng

Cover Design by Andrew Feng and Peter Feng

Cover Sketch by Andrew Feng

Cover Digital Ink by Peter Feng

Typesetting by Peter Feng

Stories in this book are works of fiction. Characters, places, names and events are either the product of the author's imagination or are used fictitiously, and any resemblance to actual persons, living or dead, business establishments, events, or locals is entirely coincidental.

First Printing: 2015-08-01

ISBN: 978-0-9938371-5-9

Digital ISBN: 978-0-9938371-6-6

www.t-u-m.net

Jack

Dr. Green

Cool-Doo

Sleepy-Doo

If you have read TUM, you know who we are.

If you haven't read it, and you want to know the

adventure of Jack and his gang,

please read TUM — The Unmoved Mover.

www.t-u-m.net

Contents

What Is a TUM Way ?

A TUM Way means

a super comic way!

Andrew

Why does TUM Way mean super comic way?

Originally, tum is an informal or childish word for stomach.

In 2013, TUM was used as the title of my children's novel, *TUM, which is a story about brotherhood and the fact that "with great power comes great responsibility."*

In the novel,

I created a new meaning for TUM.

It means super.

For example, "I have a TUM power" means "I have a super power". "You are TUM good" means "You are super good."

Why?

The reason is that TUM can be an acronym for "The Unmoved Mover," which is a philosophical concept described by Aristotle as a primary cause or "mover" of all the motion in the universe.

Wikipedia, the free encyclopedia
http://en.wikipedia.org/wiki/Unmoved_mover

In our books, my

dad and I always use comics to

tell the stories or elaborate a theory or a

methodology. That's why the TUM way is a super

comic way, a way that brings out your passion for

creative writing, a way that makes writing fun!

In this book,

I play Jack, and my dad, Peter,

plays Dr. Green.

Now, let's see how to rewrite fables

in a TUM Way!

Existing Fable KI

I know! It helps us improve our comprehension and writing skills. We can learn how to capture key information about an existing story into a KI, and then use this KI as a structure to create a new and original story.

Inspired by:

Write On Q Program
and
"What's the Gist?" Summary Writing
for Struggling Adolescent Writers
by Nancy Frey, Douglas Fisher, and Ted Hernandez
(Voice from the Middle, Volume 11 Number 2, December 2003)

TUM great,

Cool-Doo!

No!

A KI is "Key Information."

In our case, the KI is the key information of the fable.

Inspired by:

Write On Q Program
and
"What's the Gist?" Summary Writing
for Struggling Adolescent Writers
by Nancy Frey, Douglas Fisher, and Ted Hernandez
(Voice from the Middle, Volume 11 Number 2, December 2003)

That's correct.

To find a KI of a story,

we are going to look at the

overall story and pull out key

information about characters,

setting, conflict, result, and

moral.

I have a chart for you guys to fill out in order to

finish the KI. It makes your work

TUM easy.

Inspired by:

Write On Q Program
and
"What's the Gist?" Summary Writing
for Struggling Adolescent Writers
by Nancy Frey, Douglas Fisher, and Ted Hernandez
(Voice from the Middle, Volume 11 Number 2, December 2003)

Existing Fable KI

1	Title		
2	Characters	Name	
		Traits	
		Name	
		Traits	
3	Setting	Where?	
		When?	
4	Conflict	Objective	
		Incompatibility	
		Why?	
5	Result		
6	Moral		

That's

a TUM good idea!

The Tortoise and the Hare is one

of Aesop's Fables. Aesop's Fables, or the

Aesopica, is a collection of fables credited to

Aesop, a slave and storyteller believed to

have lived in ancient Greece between

620 BC and 560 BC.

Resources and References:
Wikipedia, the free encyclopedia
http://en.wikipedia.org/wiki/Aesop

My

favorite part is when the

hare fell asleep.

Anyway, remember,

to work out a good KI,

use as few words as possible

to create a phrase or a simple

sentence telling the most

important information. No

unnecessary adjectives and

adverbs are needed.

OK, let's start from the title.

Inspired by:

Write On Q Program
and
"What's the Gist?" Summary Writing
for Struggling Adolescent Writers
by Nancy Frey, Douglas Fisher, and Ted Hernandez
(Voice from the Middle,
Volume 11 Number 2, December 2003)

Nice job, Jack. Now, it's the fun part.

The conflict!

The conflict is an inherent incompatibility between the objectives of two or more characters. Conflict creates tension and interest in a story by adding doubt as to the outcome.

So, what's the conflict of this story?

Resources and References:
Wikipedia, the free encyclopedia
http://en.wikipedia.org/wiki/Conflict_(narrative)

Hold on a second. What's inherent incompatibility?

Good question, Jack.
It just means that
the characters are not naturally compatible.
For example, the tortoise and the hare don't
run at the same speed. The tortoise is
slow, while the hare is fast.

Oh.

Wait a minute. That's the ending.

The conflict should include objective, incompatibility, and reason.

The objective of the tortoise and hare is to win the race.

The incompatibility is that Tortoise is slow; Hare is fast.

Why did they have a race? Hare challenged Tortoise.

Great job, Jack!

You are catching on very quickly.

Now, let's take a look at the KI chart of

The Tortoise and the Hare.

		Existing Fable KI	
1	Title	The Tortoise and the Hare	
2	Characters	Name	Tortoise
		Traits	slow
		Name	Hare
		Traits	fast
3	Setting	Where?	forest
		When?	a day in the past
4	Conflict	Objective	win race
		Incompatibility	Tortoise is slow. Hare is fast.
		Why?	Hare challenged Tortoise.
5	Result	Hare wanted to embarrass Tortoise, pretended to nap, fell asleep, Tortoise won.	
6	Moral	Slow and steady wins the race.	

New Story KI

We'll use the KI of "The Tortoise and the Hare" as a structure to work out a new story KI.

You'll need to change everything except for the moral. Do research on the Internet, use your imaginations, think outside the box, and the sky is the limit. One thing is important: cite the information you find on the web. We'll talk about it another time.

The 2nd Day...

Good job, Jack!

Let's see what you have here.

This is

the KI of my new story.

New Story KI			
1	Title	Lamppost and Roly-Poly	
2	Characters	Name	Lamppost
		Traits	thin and eats slowly
		Name	Roly-Poly
		Traits	chubby and eats fast
3	Setting	Where?	school
		When?	lunchtime
4	Conflict	Objective	win eating contest
		Incompatibility	Lamppost is slow. Roly-Poly is fast.
		Why?	decide who pay lunch
5	Result	Roly-Poly danced, went to washroom, Lamppost won the contest.	
6	Moral	Slow and steady wins the race.	

Dress-ups
+
Sentence Openers

Now, everyone has drafted your story and I can see all of you have TUM good ideas!

To turn your good idea into a good story, not only do you need to **check spelling and grammar**, but you also need to **dressup your writing**. Type "how to dress up writing" on the Internet, you can find a lot of resources and references. Here are some dress-ups I found:

1. Because

For example: Jack had no time to think <u>because</u> he knew he had to win this game.

2. Strong Verb

For example: The two Zs <u>zoomed</u> into space, chasing Jack and his gang.

3. "-ly" Adverb

For example: The familiar music played <u>gloomily</u>.

4. Quality Adjective

For example: A bird passed by and plopped a <u>stinky</u> dropping on Jr. Z's nose.

5. Who/Which

For example: Jack, <u>who</u> aced his test, happily ran home.

6. When/While/ Where/As/Since/If/ Although

For example: Cool-Doo pretended to be asleep <u>as</u> Jack approached him.

7. Interesting Dialogue

For example: "Nice job! I bet it can win out over Jr.Z's stink bombs."

I got it.
Instead of just writing "Jack is angry", it's more fun to write: Furiously waving fists above his inflated head, Jack screamed out loud, "I'm not angry! I'm just the opposite of calm!"

Resources and References of Dress-up Types:

Teaching Writing: Structure and Style
http://www.cambriansd.org/cms/lib07/CA01902282/Centricity/Domain/316/Dress-ups_
Sentence-openers0001.pdf

BBS-Dress-ups
schools.sd68.bc.ca/RAND/div4/Worksheets/BSS%20Dress-ups.doc

Write On Q - Reference Term 3

Speaking of sentence openers, I found eleven types on the Internet. Here are 9 common ones of them:

1. Subject

For example: <u>The chip crumbs</u> went flying and splattered on Cool-Doo's face.

2. Prepositional

For example: <u>On</u> the front of the conveyer belt, were giant presses that could crush an eighteen-wheeler truck full of gold and silver bricks until it was as thin as paper.

3. Adverb

For example: <u>Suddenly</u>, black clouds filled the sky over the weatherman.

4. Adjective

For example: <u>Sad</u> about being alone in the house, Jack turned on the computer and started playing games.

5. Clausal (where, when, while, as, since, if, although, because)

For example: <u>As</u> they stepped through the hole, they found themselves on the pool deck of the control dome again.

6. VSS (very short sentence = less than five words)

For example: <u>"Correct!" the machine answered.</u>

7. "ed"

For example: <u>Startled</u> by Jack's kung-fu dance, the shark froze, its eyes widened, and all of a sudden, it swam away.

8. "ing"

For example: <u>Singing</u> in a high tone, Cool-Doo gripped the mike with shaking hands.

9. Appositive

For example: <u>A happy boy</u>, Jack, bounded around in the house.

Resources and References of Sentence Opener Types:

How to Vary Sentence Beginnings
by Ann Moore, Demand Media
http://classroom.synonym.com/vary-sentence-beginnings-4155.html

Write On Q - Reference Term 2

Hi, readers!

The three boys did TUM wonderful work on their writings of new stories, and the more they wrote, the more they loved creative writing.

Here are six new stories written by the three boys based on six existing fables.

Finish the exercise after each story and write your own version of a new story.

To let you practice doing research, I just listed the title of each existing fable. You can find the content on the Internet.

Have
TUM FUN!

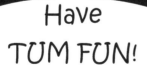

Resources and References of Fables:
Write On Q - Source Text Term 2

Wait a minute! Before you have fun on rewriting, there is one very important thing you should pay close attention to:

Don't PLAGIARIZE!

But you may wonder: If my idea is inspired by some information that can be found in many resources, do I have to give an acknowledgement for everything I write?

Dr. Margaret Procter (University of Toronto Coordinator, Writing Support) elaborated the theory: "*I didn't know anything about the subject until I started this paper. Do I have to give an acknowledgement for every point I make? You're safer to over-reference than to skimp. But you can cut down the clutter by recognizing that some ideas are "common knowledge" in the field—that is, taken for granted by people knowledgeable about the topic.*"

To find more information about how to avoid plagiarizing— meaning, copying other people's work—you can read Dr. Margaret Procter's article online at: www.writing. utoronto.ca/advice/using-sources/how-not-to- plagiarize.

Now, you can have fun!

{New Story - 1}

Roly-Poly and Lamppost

Source Fable Title: The Tortoise and the Hare
(Please find the content on the Internet.)

In a noisy classroom filled with blabbering kids, notes, and paper airplanes, there stood a new student named Eric by the door with his teacher.

"Meet our new student, Eric!" the teacher announced.

Eric was listening to music with his headphones on and was shaking his chubby body in a whimsical way.

"He looks like a dancing Roly-Poly toy," the students whispered to each other. And that was true. Eric was as round as a

Roly-Poly toy. So, that was how Eric got his nickname right away, Roly-Poly.

There was also another student in the class who was the complete opposite of Eric, named Tim. He was very thin like a lamppost, which was the name his classmates always called him. When Lamppost ate, he always took slow and even bites of his food.

The lunch bell rang, so everyone scrambled into the cafeteria. Just after Lamppost bought his lunch, he and Roly-Poly bumped into each other. Both of their lunches fell down and messily splattered on the floor.

"Hey!" exclaimed Roly-Poly. "You made me drop my lunch! I'll have to buy another one, but you have to pay for it! You're unbelievable!"

"I would be grateful if you would buy me a lunch," Lamppost replied slowly, although he was angry on the inside.

The two argued and argued, until Roly-Poly came up with a plan. "Wait, I have an idea! We'll have an eating contest. Whoever eats the most burgers in ten minutes wins and the losing person will have to pay for all the burgers."

Lamppost agreed reluctantly.

"But, I doubt you'll win against me!" Roly-Poly laughed as he patted his round stomach. "This is my lethal weapon!"

So, the two boys sat at a table, staring at each other, with students watching intently, as if it was a draw in the middle of an old town in the Wild West.

Roly-Poly hammered the table and shouted, "Let's start!"

Lamppost shrugged and murmured, "OK."

Roly-Poly gobbled and gnashed at his burgers, while Lamppost took slow and even bites.

After about a minute, Roly-Poly stopped eating and relaxed. "Look at how slow you eat! It will take all day before you finish eating your first burger!" Roly-Poly teased.

Suddenly, someone turned on the jukebox in the cafeteria, and music filled the room. "Hey, this is my favorite song!" Roly-Poly exclaimed. He put down his second burger and started dancing to the music winningly.

Lamppost kept eating without looking at anything except the burger in his skinny hands.

Very soon, Roly-Poly stopped dancing and clutched his stomach. "Oof, I don't feel so good. Ugh." He raced to the bathroom and made a lot of unpleasant noises. Ten minutes passed. Lamppost finished his second burger.

Just at that moment, Roly-Poly waltzed out of the bathroom. He suddenly stopped. He looked at the timer, his burgers, and then at Lamppost's burgers. "Ahhh! I can't believe I'll have to pay for the lunch!"

Moral: Slow and steady wins the race.

PRACTICE - 1

Find 3 examples for each type of dress-up:

- Dress-up Type 1: _____

    1. _____

    2. _____

    3. _____

- Dress-up Type 2: _____

    1. _____

    2. _____

    3. _____

- Dress-up Type 3: _____

    1. _____

    2. _____

    3. _____

- Dress-up Type 4: _____

    1. _____

    2. _____

    3. _____

Find 3 examples of different sentence openers:

1. _____

Sample sentence: _____

_____

_____

_____

2. _____

Sample sentence: _____

_____

_____

_____

3. _____

Sample sentence: _____

_____

_____

_____

Finish the KI chart on the next page and write your own new story.

	Existing Fable	New Story
KI		

		Existing Fable	New Story
Title			
Characters	Name		
	Traits		
	Name		
	Traits		
Setting	Where?		
	When?		
Conflict	Objective		
	Incompatibility		
	Why?		
Result			
Moral			

{New Story - 2}

The City Car
and
the Country Car

Source Fable Title:
The Town Mouse and the Country Mouse
(Please find the content on the Internet.)

Far away in the countryside, the sun

perched on the fluffy clouds like a big, golden

pumpkin resting in cotton candy. Grassy

fields carried on endlessly as the day went

on. A dirt road ran from the horizon and cut

through rolling hills of vast green trees. All

of a sudden, a cloud of dust appeared on the

road. With a screech, the dust disappeared,

and there stood a city car looking confused.

"Hmmm...is this where he is? I think I didn't

follow directions carefully."

At that moment, an old, rusty car slowly drove out of his garage.

"Howdy, friend! You drive pretty fast! You came much earlier than I expected. Well, this is the countryside."

The city car made a puzzled face, looked around, and then remarked, "Oh. I thought I was off course. So, this is your place."

The country car smiled and gave a small chuckle. "Yep, this is my place. I'll give you a tour of the countryside."

The two cars rumbled down the dirt road, spitting dust here and there. Just then, a flock of ducks waddled across the road. The two cars stopped, but the city car honked its horn. "Beep beep! Hey, ducks! This isn't a zoo, this is a road. Go back to your zoo!" he yelled.

As the ducks quickly shuffled away, the country car scowled at his friend. "Hey, fella. This is the countryside. 'Mi casa su casa.' Well, the same rule applies here. 'My road is the ducks road.' Now that's life in the countryside."

The city car shook his head in disgust. "Ugh, this is boring! There are just farms, fields, barns, trees, and ducks here! Is there anything else!?"

The country car grinned and said calmly, "Well, there are cows, too."

The city car rolled his headlights and grunted. "The point is, there's nothing fun in the countryside, because the most exciting thing we did was watching a group of birds walk across a road. Let's go to the city. I bet you'll have a great time there."

The city car rumbled its motor, shook its body, and pranced up and down, making the windows vibrate furiously. Away he zipped, down the road with clouds of dirt puffing out beneath him.

Suddenly, he screeched to a halt and looked behind him. "Hey, what's the holdup?" he shouted.

"Uhhh, got a few engine problems here." the country car cried back as he sputtered smoke continuously in small puffs. Suddenly, he seemed to be working again. "OK, I got it. Let's go to this city of yours!"

The two cars drove and drove until they finally reached the city.

"Ahhh, look at the marvelous sun!" the city car said to the country car.

The country car beamed and replied, "Yeah, it looks like a big, golden pumpkin, floating in the sky." The city car laughed. "Ha ha ha! Boy, you're funny. Actually, it's like a newly-polished penny, and since it glows so much, it appears to resemble the rich, glorious sun."

The country car frowned and scoffed, "I still prefer my golden pumpkin idea."

The city car rushed forward and yelled back, "Never mind! Let's go, already."

Streetlights stood sentinel along the road. The two friends passed a towering skyscraper. Startled by the building's height, the country car shuddered. "Yikes! This house is so tall! Does it ever topple down?"

The city car chuckled at his friend. "It's called a business skyscraper. And no, these types of buildings do not usually fall down. But, the stock prices for the company in this skyscraper could topple. Ha ha. City humour."

The country car backed away from the building. "Then we should get away from those stock prices!" he said with a quivering voice.

The city car roared with laughter. "You're hilarious! Come on, let's go to the street concert to settle you down."

However, the street concert did not make the country car settle down. As they got closer to the concert, the music became louder and louder. Soon, the two cars found themselves surrounded by ear-piercing music.

"Ahhh! It's too loud here!" the country car shrieked. He felt like his windows were going to burst into smithereens.

"It's all part of the show!" the city car boomed. "But, if you can't stand this, let's go somewhere else! We have lots of fantastic places here. How about the cinema? Hurry, we don't want to be stuck in a traffic jam!"

The country car made a puzzled face and asked, "What's a traffic jam? I like strawberry jam."

The city car smirked and said, "Oh, it's a very different jam, my friend. A ton of cars crowded on the road, busy streets, lots of honking and beeping, and cars stuck in a big, messy line."

The country car sighed and shook his head. "Patience is a virtue. And so is this."

The two cars drove through the city hurriedly. The friends maneuvered themselves through a rabble of cars, constantly being beeped and honked at. They passed a small accident by the edge of the road. "Yikes! Driving in the city looks pretty dangerous!" the country car stammered.

Just at that moment, a vehicle bumped into the city car. "Hey! Look what you did to my paint!" the city car hollered at the vehicle.

The country car shuddered in fright and frowned at the city car.

"Can we pull over for a second?" he

asked his still-angry friend.

"Sure, but we have to hurry," the city car said. "The traffic's only gonna get worse."

They pulled to the side of the road as other cars whizzed by. "Thanks for inviting me to the city with you, friend," the country car said. He had to shout to be heard over the highway noise. "It's fun and exciting here, but I don't really feel comfortable in the city. I'm just gonna go back to the countryside. I prefer my simple life."

Moral: A simple life is sometimes better.

PRACTICE

Find 3 examples for each type of dress-up:

- Dress-up Type 1: _____

    1. _____

    2. _____

    3. _____

- Dress-up Type 2: _____

    1. _____

    2. _____

    3. _____

- Dress-up Type 3: _____

    1. _____

    2. _____

    3. _____

- Dress-up Type 4: _____

    1. _____

    2. _____

    3. _____

Find 3 examples of different sentence openers:

1. _____

Sample sentence: _____

_____

_____

_____

2. _____

Sample sentence: _____

_____

_____

_____

3. _____

Sample sentence: _____

_____

_____

_____

Finish the KI chart on the next page and write your own new story.

KI

		Existing Fable	New Story
Title			
Characters	Name		
	Traits		
	Name		
	Traits		
Setting	Where?		
	When?		
Conflict	Objective		
	Incompatibility		
	Why?		
Result			
Moral			

{New Story - 3}

The Alien Who Cried Space Tornado

Source Fable Title: The Boy Who Cried Wolf
(Please find the content on the Internet.)

In a galaxy far, far away, there lived a young alien called Shorty who always wore a pair of blue boots and whose job was to watch out for lethal space tornados for his community's space snail farm. Space snails were the aliens' main food and space tornados traveled around in the universe to sweep away anything they passed.

Luckily, aliens invented the Space Tornado Evaporator Gun (STEG) which could destroy the space tornados. Shorty was instructed to patrol the space snail farm in a boring pod and step on the alarm button to send a signal to the other aliens when his monitor showed a tornado was coming. When the aliens received the signal, they would snatch their STEGs and evaporate the space tornados.

Every day, Shorty felt bored and wanted some company.

One day, he stepped on the alarm button with his blue boot to signal the other aliens. They received the alarm, hastily grabbed their STEGs, and zipped to Shorty heavily armed. *Clink-clank-clink-clank-clink-clank-cli* — They suddenly screeched to a halt. "Where's the space tornado?" they questioned Shorty.

The little alien frowned. "I just felt really bored and wanted some company. Sorry." The aliens looked at each other and then at the young alien sympathetically. "We accept your apology, but don't do that again, Shorty." Shorty nodded.

For a long time he did not trick the aliens, but one day he felt more bored than last time. Shorty knew he shouldn't, but he alerted the other aliens. They hurriedly sprinted to Shorty with their STEGs. Again they discovered that there was no space tornado. "You must stop immediately!" an alien scolded. "This is not funny anymore."

Shorty sighed. "OK."

Just after the aliens left, Shorty checked his monitor and spied a space tornado zooming toward him. He stomped on the alert-signal button. The alien inhabitants started getting their STEGs, but then they stopped. They thought it was another trick. However, they suddenly saw a little object whirling ahead of them. They ran to the space tornado with their STEGs. Soon, with a big ZAP, the space tornado was destroyed.

However, they could not find Shorty. All they discovered was the alien's blue boot, lying on the space snail farm.

Moral: This shows how liars are rewarded — even if they tell the truth, no one believes them.

PRACTICE

Find 3 examples for each type of dress-up:

- Dress-up Type 1: _____

    1. _____

    2. _____

    3. _____

- Dress-up Type 2: _____

    1. _____

    2. _____

    3. _____

- Dress-up Type 3: _____

    1. _____

    2. _____

    3. _____

- Dress-up Type 4: _____

    1. _____

    2. _____

    3. _____

Find 3 examples of different sentence openers:

1. _____

Sample sentence: _____

_____

_____

_____

2. _____

Sample sentence: _____

_____

_____

_____

3. _____

Sample sentence: _____

_____

_____

_____

Finish the KI chart on the next page and write your own new story.

KI		
	Existing Fable	New Story
Title		
Characters Name		
Traits		
Name		
Traits		
Setting Where?		
When?		
Conflict Objective		
Incompatibility		
Why?		
Result		
Moral		

{New Story - 4}

The Boy's Backpack

Source Fable Title:
Grandmother's Table adapted from Brothers Grimm
(Please find the content on the Internet.)

On a warm, summer day, a boy named

Aiden was playing cheerfully in his front

yard. Soon, he found a backpack lying on the

sidewalk. Aiden looked around, but nobody

was in sight. He picked it up and found an

address tag attached to it. Aiden read the

address and exclaimed, "Awww, jeez. This guy

lives ten blocks from here. Whatever. He'll

buy a backpack sooner or later." Aiden tossed

the backpack into a pile of junk in his garage.

The next day, while Aiden was walking

home from school, he noticed some of his

friends playing in a park. Wanting to join them, he dropped his backpack and played with his friends. After a while, Aiden resumed his walk home, not realizing that he forgot his backpack at the park! As soon as he arrived at his house, Aiden plopped down on his chair, picked up a pencil, and just as he was about to write his homework, he glanced at the door and angrily dropped it. "Darn it, I forgot my backpack at the park!" Aiden cried. "Forgot...backpack...at...park...go...all...the...way...back...and...get...it..." he muttered as he pulled on his shoes.

Just at that moment, the doorbell rang. "Coming," Aiden mumbled. As Aiden opened the door, he found a little boy clutching a backpack in his hands — Aiden's backpack.

"Are you Aiden?" he asked.

Aiden smiled. "Yeah, yeah I am." He felt extremely grateful and took his backpack. "Thanks a lot."

The amiable boy grinned, "No problem," he said and bounded down the steps and jogged away.

At this moment, something bothered Aiden. Aiden hastily opened his garage and tossed through the pile of junk until he spotted the backpack he found yesterday. "Time to do something in return."

After a long walk, Aiden finally reached the person's house. He carried the backpack up the steps and rang the doorbell. A boy opened the door. Aiden handed the backpack to him.

"I've been looking for this. Thanks a billion!" The boy cheerfully replied.

The last rays of sunlight shone on the boy's backpack, Aiden's brown hair, and maybe on a tiny smile that Aiden had as he disappeared down the road.

Moral: Treat other people the way you want to be treated.

PRACTICE

Find 3 examples for each type of dress-up:

- Dress-up Type 1: _____

    1. _____

    2. _____

    3. _____

- Dress-up Type 2: _____

    1. _____

    2. _____

    3. _____

- Dress-up Type 3: _____

    1. _____

    2. _____

    3. _____

- Dress-up Type 4: _____

    1. _____

    2. _____

    3. _____

Find 3 examples of different sentence openers:

1. _____

Sample sentence: _____

_____

_____

_____

2. _____

Sample sentence: _____

_____

_____

_____

3. _____

Sample sentence: _____

_____

_____

_____

Finish the KI chart on the next page and write your own new story.

	Existing Fable	New Story
KI		
Title		
Characters — Name		
Traits		
Name		
Traits		
Setting — Where?		
When?		
Conflict — Objective		
Incompatibility		
Why?		
Result		
Moral		

{New Story - 5}

The Computer Fan and the Monitor

Source Fable Title: The Bat and the Nightingale
(Please find the content on the Internet.)

"Whew! Finally he left to get a snack. I'm so tired," the computer fan sighed, exhausted. The sweat ran down his blades as he wiped the dust out of his eyes. A reflection of a computer monitor shone on one of the drops, attracting the fan's attention. He found himself craning his neck to eye the large, majestic monitor who was staring down at him. "I can't wait to see what's going to happen next in his game!" the monitor said proudly. The fan looked up from his break and sarcastically scoffed, "Exciting, isn't it?"

"Yes, indeed. The boy plays all because of me. I show him all the games." the monitor gloated.

Squinting his eyes, the fan frowned at the monitor. "What do you mean?"

The monitor beamed and replied, "Oh, you know. Standing up here, shining brightly like a movie star. Yep, I'm the big guy, my little midget."

The computer fan looked back down and muttered, "We'll see about that."

The boy came back, hopped on his chair and started playing his game. His fingers flew over the keyboard, constantly tapping keys and clicking the mouse. The monitor flashed and made a variety of sounds, fascinating the boy. Suddenly, the screen blacked out. The boy gasped and shook the monitor furiously. "What! How? I almost completed level eighty-three! This monitor is new! Do I have to toss it out and buy a new one again?" With that, he hopped off his chair and bounded away.

The monitor yelled in a panick, "Ahhh! Don't go away! Don't throw me out!"

Below him, the fan winked and teased, "Hey, big guy. What's the problem?"

The anxious monitor sobbed, "My screen blacked out because the CPU got too hot and shut down automatically. Now the boy's gonna throw me out! It's absolutely unfair! It's not my fault!"

The fan mischievously grinned and asked, "Do you know why, Mr. Big?" The monitor shook his head and looked at the little fan curiously. "Well, the reason that the CPU got too hot was that I stopped working. You see, although you are big and you shine like a star, I have to spend my whole time cooling the CPU off, making sure it doesn't get too hot. It's like a junk yard down here — messy wires tangled everywhere, with layers of greasy dust and dirt. Without my hard work, everything in this box may burn out."

The monitor grimaced and apologized. "Sorry, buddy. I underestimated you. I just thought that I was the one in the spotlight, since I show all the games."

The fan spun his blades in agreement

with a whirring sound. "Apology accepted.
Let's work together." With that, the fan
whirled and swished in the machine, until
it got cooler. Then, the computer turned
back on. The game was still on, so music and
sounds burst out of the speaker. The boy
heard the noise and dashed back excitedly.
"Hey, my computer is still alive!" Eagerly, he
started playing the game with a smile as big
as the moon. The monitor glanced at the fan,
seeing both of themselves grinning in the
reflection of the fan's drop of sweat.

Moral 1: Working together in harmony
may produce a better result than working
alone.

Moral 2: Appreciate the contributions
of others, however small they are.

PRACTICE

Find 3 examples of each type of dress-up:

- Dress-up Type 1: _____

    1. _____

    2. _____

    3. _____

- Dress-up Type 2: _____

    1. _____

    2. _____

    3. _____

- Dress-up Type 3: _____

    1. _____

    2. _____

    3. _____

- Dress-up Type 4: _____

    1. _____

    2. _____

    3. _____

Find 3 examples for different sentence openers:

1. _____

Sample sentence: _____

_____

_____

_____

2. _____

Sample sentence: _____

_____

_____

_____

3. _____

Sample sentence: _____

_____

_____

_____

Finish the KI chart on the next page and write your own new story.

KI		
	Existing Fable	New Story
Title		
Characters — Name		
Traits		
Name		
Traits		
Setting — Where?		
When?		
Conflict — Objective		
Incompatibility		
Why?		
Result		
Moral		

{New Story - 6}

The Large Kite and the Small Pair of Scissors

Source Fable Title: The Lion and the Mouse
(Please find the content on the Internet.)

There was once a small pair of scissors.

He was bounding around playfully in a

playground, when all of a sudden, he got

stuck in a puddle of mud! The pair of scissors

squirmed vigorously as he tried to pull himself

out of the mud. However, the more he

struggled, the deeper he sank. Then, right out

of the blue, came a large, majestic kite, sailing

in the sky. He bobbed as the wind carried

him. Being high above, the world seemed like

the kite's own realm.

"Ahoy there!" the kite hollered at the pair of scissors. "Do you need any help?"

The pair of scissors was relieved. "Yes! Help me!"

"Hold on to my string tightly when I tell you to!" the kite yelled. He drifted slightly downward and let his string settle to the ground. "Now!" he ordered. With no hesitation, the pair of scissors seized the kite's string and held on. Slowly, he rose out of the mud as the kite waggled up.

"Thanks," the pair of scissors said. "I promise I'll help you someday."

The kite laughed. "You? Help me? Oh, sure!" He floated away, still roaring with laughter. "Classic," the kite muttered.

The next day, the kite was taking a happy stroll in the sky when suddenly he flew into a tree and got tangled in a thin branch. Then, he saw the same pair of scissors that he saved yesterday, playing by the tree. The kite felt awkward asking for help, so he did not make a sound. The kite wiggled, causing leaves to fall down from the branch. A leaf fell on the pair of scissors. He looked up, noticing the troubled kite. "Oh, it's you! Here, I'll help."

The kite tried to sound like he just saw him.

"You again? How could you help me? You couldn't fly or have the strength to push me off this tree! Go call a bird or something. You're useless!"

The pair of scissors ignored the kite and started climbing the tree. He reached the kite.

"I already told you, go take a hike!" the kite scolded.

"Well, you're wrong," the pair of scissors replied. With a *snip*, he cut the branch off the tree with his blades. The kite flew back into the sky. The kite's frown turned upside down. "Oh, so that's what you can do! Sorry I underestimated you."

The pair of scissors grinned. "It's OK! One good turn always deserves another."

Moral 1: One good turn always deserves another.

Moral 2: Never underestimate a small person's ability.

PRACTICE

Find 3 examples for each type of dress-up:

- Dress-up Type 1: _____

    1. _____

    2. _____

    3. _____

- Dress-up Type 2: _____

    1. _____

    2. _____

    3. _____

- Dress-up Type 3: _____

    1. _____

    2. _____

    3. _____

- Dress-up Type 4: _____

    1. _____

    2. _____

    3. _____

Find 3 examples of different sentence openers:

1. _____

Sample sentence: _____

_____

_____

_____

2. _____

Sample sentence: _____

_____

_____

_____

3. _____

Sample sentence: _____

_____

_____

_____

Finish the KI chart on the next page and write your own new story.

KI

		Existing Fable	New Story
Title			
Characters	Name		
	Traits		
	Name		
	Traits		
Setting	Where?		
	When?		
Conflict	Objective		
	Incompatibility		
	Why?		
Result			
Moral			

Resources and References

The Write On Q Program - Creative Writing

Tracy Ostwald-Kowald - *Rethinking Fables and Fairy Tales: A Story Retelling Activity* http://www.connectionsacademy.com/blog/posts/2013-12-13/Rethinking-Fables-and-Fairy-Tales-A-Story-Retelling-Activity.aspx

Rewriting an existing story (fable) to fit it within my fantasy universe http://writers.stackexchange.com/questions/9731/rewriting-an-existing-story-fable-to-fit-it-within-my-fantasy-universe

Dr. Margaret Procter
University of Toronto Coordinator, Writing Support
How Not to Plagiarize
Updated 14 July 2010
www.writing.utoronto.ca/advice/using-sources/how-not-to-plagiarize

Ann Moore, Demand Media
How to Vary Sentence Beginnings
http://classroom.synonym.com/vary-sentence-beginnings-4155.html

Wikipedia, the free encyclopedia
http://en.wikipedia.org/wiki/Unmoved_mover
http://en.wikipedia.org/wiki/Conflict_(narrative)
http://en.wikipedia.org/wiki/Aesop

The idea of writing this book is inspired by:
- *The Write On Q Program - Creative Writing*   www.writeonq.ca
- Tracy Ostwald-Kowald - *Rethinking Fables and Fairy Tales: A Story Retelling Activity*   http://www.connectionsacademy.com/blog/posts/2013-12-13/Rethinking-Fables-and-Fairy-Tales-A-Story-Retelling-Activity.aspx
- *Rewriting an existing story (fable) to fit it within my fantasy universe* http://writers.stackexchange.com/questions/9731/rewriting-an-existing-story-fable-to-fit-it-within-my-fantasy-universe

There are ideas in this book based on common knowledge or methodology in the field of creative writing that can be found in too many resources. It is impossible for us to list all resources and references. We sincerely appreciate everyone who is passionate about creative writing and shares their knowledge and methodology with others.

If you do find some extra resources in this book that need to be cited or you think some citations are not proper, please do not hesitate to contact us at: info@t-u-m.net.

Other Fun Books
by Andrew Feng and Peter Feng

Do you get along with your brother?

Jack doesn't!

Although he has always expected to have a brother to play with, he finds his dream of brotherhood shattered after he gets a really "special" one. This special one always impresses Jack's parents. Plus, this special one also has a special friend of his own, and things always stir up crazily.

Finally, a chance comes for Jack to impress his parents. His hometown is placed in danger while he and the other two special guys are in a space camp, and he only has one night left to become the hero. But, of course, his "special" brother also wants to be the hero.

The clock is ticking...can they make it?

(www.t-u-m.net)

" *A lively adventure that charms and delights!* "
- KIRKUS REVIEWS

Learn math while you are laughing!

Cool-Doo Math is a comic series with all the

main characters from *TUM — The Unmoved Mover*.

Word problems are usually boring for most kids.

Cool-Doo Math turns those knotty problems

into funny comics.

Kids will find math so interesting!

Visit www.cool-doo.com for details.

About the Author

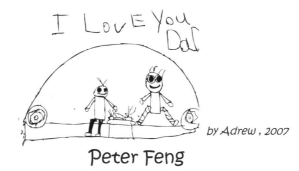

by Adrew, 2007

Peter Feng

Peter is a realtor working in Great Tronto Area. He is neither a writer nor a professional illustrator. In 2008, his wife had a miscarriage that made his son Andrew very upset because he always dreamed of having a little brother. To cheer up his son, Peter created an imaginary brother Cool-Doo for Andrew and started creating Cool-Doo stories together with him. With the passion for creating a new family tradition, Peter and his son started learning creative writing from books, the Internet, teachers, writers and editors. With the help and support of family, friends and professional editors, Peter and Andrew published a children's novel, *TUM — The Unmoved Mover*, and a math comic series, *Cool-Doo Math*.

Peter loves the unmeasured, vast expanse of the ocean. He always sees himself as a sailor in the crow's nest looking beyond the horizon, a sailor who never gives up exploring and searching for a new continent.

by Adrew, 2009

About the Author

Andrew Feng

"Myths can be true; fairy tales can be true; even lies can be true. So, why not my dreams?"

Who made up this quote?

Andrew Feng did!

Born on a snowy day, he has always loved drawing doodles from his imagination, whether it's about ordinary Joes traveling around the world or extraordinary guys trying to defeat super villains.

Now, he enjoys drawing comics, reading, writing, swiming, playing the guitar, table tennis, tennis, and basketball, all with his best buddies.

Andrew is not sure what to be when he grows up, but he does know one thing — he will be an awesordinary (awesome + ordinary) guy!

(2015)

Postface

Andrew and I hope to use funny comics to elaborate some basic methodology about creative writing so that kids can learn while laughing.

We also hope that our effort will inspire other kids and parents to discover their passion in life and to be creative — especially for those new immigrants like us who move to a new country pursuing a new and better life, but facing a lot of challenges. The largest challenge for new immigrants is language. I always get nervous when I speak or write English, even when I am typing this postface. But one little spark in my heart ignites my enthusiasm for writing: to make my son happy, to create a new family tradition, to leave something behind for my descendants. Sometimes when I burn the midnight oil to ink my son's comic drawings, I imagine how excited my grandchildren will be when they read those books that their dad and grandpa wrote, and how those books can inspire them to ... Wait a minute ... Maybe they will not care; maybe it is just my dream.

I've always liked a quote by Vincent van Gogh - *"A great fire burns within me, but no one stops to warm themselves at it, and passers-by only see a wisp of smoke."*

The only splendid life you have is the moment that you really live in. Otherwise it is just a wisp of smoke drifting away. For me, the smile on my son's face when he is holding our books is one of the moments I enjoy most in my life.

- Peter Feng

35114180R00068

Made in the USA
Middletown, DE
04 February 2019